THE ONLY HOME WE KNOW

The Only Home We Know

poems

Robin Chapman

TEBOT BACH • HUNTINGTON BEACH • CALIFORNIA • 2019

Cover art: *Light in the Forest*, acrylic by Robin Chapman
Author photo credit: Will Zarwell
Book design: Gray Dog Press, Spokane, WA

ISBN-10: 1-939678-57-9
ISBN-13: 978-1-939678-57-7
Library of Congress Control Number: 2019934615

A Tebot Bach book.
Tebot Bach, Welsh for little teapot, is a Nonprofit Public Benefit
Corporation, which sponsors workshops, forums, lectures, and
publications. Tebot Bach books are distributed by Small Press
Distribution, Armadillo and Ingram.

The Tebot Bach Mission: Advancing literacy, strengthening
community, and transforming life experiences with the power of
poetry through readings, workshops, and publications.

This book is made possible by a generous donation from Steven R. and Lera B. Smith.

www.tebotbach.org

Contents

I. Tally

II. The Alphabet of Time

III. Gravitational Waves

I
Tally

The Tension of Opposites

So I'm working to remember to move both ways—
up against a wall of Googled news, to study
the movements of planets above the lodgepoles—
how Jupiter brushes by the full moon!—
and yet another I-went-to-the woods-and-felt
sort-of-religious poem, even if true, carries
the thought that the next should be about burgers
and sweet potato fries, or overheard talk
among the pork producer conferees about
pleasuring sows in artificial insemination;
and from the scientist in celestial mechanics,
yes, in some billion years, our planets' orbits
will fall apart like any chaotic n-body system;
for now, love, put on your clown nose
and dance with me under the wandering planets.

Banff Centre
Dec. 25

Dear Ones—dinner of sweet potato fries
and Black Angus burgers with bloodied boxers
on TV, the puppeteer journaling her family
under the flickering fight. Circus instructors
plan their work on silks and ropes and hoops
and the 30-foot swing of the giant trapeze.
The far-flung world whispers to faces buried
in their screens. The new Creativity Center rises
sheathed in steel and glass. In my studio,
the dark outside retreats before the sluice
of podcast radio, science news, gigabytes
of music I transfer from my memory stick.
Attention is our scarcest resource—mine,
to find the mountains rising all round us,
the stars flickering beyond the drizzle of snow,
the earth in its journey turning us again
toward light, the text of good will arriving,
the red silk fluttering with its human freight.

Circles

—after Do Ho Suh's MMoCA exhibit, 2017

Drag me through space—
I'm a pipeline, a smokestack,
a dial for the burner
on the stove,
or spun round myself,
a globe.

I'm the mouth
of a black hole,
event horizon
wiped clean
of star crumbs,

enso,
zero.

Pull me down through a line—
I'm a point
split in two,
halves fleeing each other,
rushing away,
then back again.

Oh, geometry
of home—
endlessly
I turn.

Time makes of me
a spiraling thread.

Cassandra Thinks on An Old Proverb

(def: hysteresis:
a lagging of effect when forces are changed)

Look—the California aquifer's drying up
and does not replenish itself, the western plains
are heading into hardpan for generations,
the glaciers and mountain snow packs going
gone with their reservoir of water, the shade
of the pine forests dropping with their needles,
whole rivers are trickling into dust, the forests cut
cannot be rebuilt in a hundred years, the animals
lost from their haunts, the soil that gave life
blows away, oh look, look at the future we're
making I'm crying, my name is Cassandra
and again you want to throw me off the parapets,
a woman ranting hysterically about hysteresis,
an ounce of prevention now, or centuries of cure.

Jan. 6,
Banff

Dear Ones—the avalanche cannons
are going off on chinook-slicked slopes.
Listening to their distant booms I try
to imagine the sounds close up, loud
enough to trigger the tree-felling rush
of snow and ice down mountain sides—
the way those New Year's cannon fireworks
must have sounded to the blackbirds
in their roost—I wonder who set them off,
and whether they meant for five thousand
birds, in blind panic, to collide and die,
falling dead from the sky—no one
in that small Arkansas town is telling who
or why, though all must know by now
whether it was a kid's tragic prank
or some hired exterminator's culling.

Light

Here in the short mountain days of December
we can't stop looking at the 10:00 a.m. apricot light
pouring through the pines, raying the snow
in the spoked wheel of sunrise, the deep blue
shadows of pine. Bounding the ravine, two martens
trace fluid dark paths, bodies pouring in and out
of underbrush and burrows. The nuthatch climbs
the lodgepole, blue feathers and black cap.
Deer hoof-prints stitch the snow crust. At breakfast
we talked of the night sky, so deeply blue, all
the starry field that has vanished from our city eyes.
And walking home last night, moonlight cast up
from the snow lit our way, while far to the north,
auroral dark, the thousand and two visible stars,
the Milky Way, divided the year from penumbral day.
All of life spun daily past the sun, the wheeling moon,
the blue-black starfield, the wandering planets,
our bodies' clocks reset to sunrise, moon, and night.

Dreams of the Science Writers' Workshop

i.

I go naked to the Senior Center
to pick up our speaker, much
to the disapproval of the matron
and the surprise of the reporters
gathered to hear yet another
political candidate. We barely escape
with our notes.

ii.

Mummified, we stand around the table
each in our open coffin shouting out
our own particular version of truth
for our allotted hour or number of words.
Amplified, true; but hard, in my dream,
to walk-about.

iii.

What do I want to shout?
Look at the plans of our scientists
more than half a century ago
to bomb in hundred-Hiroshima units
anyone we were afraid of!
Look at our powers to make
the poisons that could kill
all life, the viruses that the birds
could spread, the gene editing
and drives that could change
the lives of species in ways we know
nothing about: look at our inventions
pouring into soil, and water, and lives;
it is not enough to be a scientist,
not enough to blow things up
or knock them out.

Ask how to be a peacemaker,
a baker, an obstetrician,
a dancer, a weaver, a musician,
a gardener, mother and father
to children, lover of life!

iv.
The headlines now fear robots
with machine intelligence.
Leonardo da Vinci: it was not enough
to make plans to improve the machines
on the rock shelf of civilization
to hurl stones and pour oil;
not enough to paint Mona Lisa
and walk beautifully about.

v.
Cortés
ordered the burning
of Montezuma's aviaries.
Our military rained down
Agent Orange for years
on the forests of Vietnam.
And now our own peaceful driving about
and heating our houses
and burning our trash
threatens to strip
the aviaries of all the world.

vi.
Don't stop
at beating our swords to ploughshares,
charge our gun-makers
with switching to tiny shot-gun houses
set up for the homeless, harmonicas,
and metal park benches,

our soldiers with making peace through art,
our oil fields with rehabilitation as parks,
shift the profits from death
to taxes for free college for all,
make of our cities gardens and aviaries
and flowered walking paths
for the bees and ourselves,
teach us
dances where all join the circle,
let the number of musicians
be as numerous as the plastic bottles
littering our shores.

January

Raven calling overhead,
red squirrel rushing from tree to tree
in the lodgepole woods, light finding
a line of snowbank here and here,
brightening a strip of bark,
reaching into our winter lives—
this morning the sun cast pink light
onto the mountaintops
as the moon, past full, set
behind their glow—and we tuned
again to the world's cycle,
finding the natural rhythm
of our day.

A warm wind

is melting the layers of snow
and the young mule deer
is foraging mouthfuls of windfalls—
branchlets re-emerge
in the shrinking crust
that an earlier Chinook
shook from the pines—
how the layers of time
accumulate, condense,
become common ground
before they slip under
the next snowfall.

3 p.m. guilty love poem in the artist's studio
—for Will

I have sent you away
to have space in the day
to write poems about
how much I love you
unstintingly, without
doubt or qualification,
and now I am feeling
incredibly bad that I
have made you go
find your own version
of play even though
when you sat down
in my chair and settled
in with your sandwich
and milk I was exceed-
ingly ticked that
you'd invaded my space
in which I planned
to compose the poem
that would have appeared
in place of this one.

Methods: A Word

And the one I've drawn, opening the dictionary,
is *self-denial*, that hair-shirt specialty of martyrs
mortifying the flesh by going without food or drink;
indeed the whole two pages offer hyphenated
options, running from the proud self-made
self-reliant self-images gracing every startup's
CEO page to self-limited self-less self-surrender
advised on the yoga workouts, displaying our species'
preoccupation with self, revolving around the axis of ego
like a maypole—self-referenced, self-centered,
self-possessed—and somewhere we add a selfie
to the profile, though it's not in Webster's yet.

Posts

—after L. Mueller's *Things*

What happened is, we grew lonely
    before our screens,
      and so we found a place where we could see

friends' faces and gave our messages
    names—what we said or shouted
      or tweeted in type no longer speech

but text, a status update,
    and what we couldn't say
      we pointed to with links—

or photographed; and because
        we wanted to connect
    with the faces that we met, we clicked

like, or added a comment and smiley face; and because
    we still made art and wanted
      to share, we did; embedded

in our century of wars, we borrowed
    language and called it
      bombing, spattering the screen

with paintings and poems, our greatest
    hits replayed on our timeline page,
      edited to step around the marketing.

The best part I almost forgot. No one forgot
    the birthday of any friend; and on
      our own day, good wishes poured in.

Banff,
Jan. 16

Dear Ones—I want to complain
there are no animals in these woods,
but that's a mistake—I'm here,
and the magpies and red squirrel,
the tracks of a nocturnal mouse,
the pee posts of the security guard's dog,
and just across the valley on Sulphur's
flank, the sighting of a cougar mother
and her cubs. Outside, a Bobcat tractor,
motor growling, clears away snow
on a gray day with low fog blanking
out the woods. The smallest flakes
descend like a swarm of gnats.
Above me a caramel roof of Douglas fir,
walls a Haida round stretched out.
And out on the ridge a butterscotch splotch
I've been staring at all morning,
wondering if one of the local cougars
could be stretched out taking a nap
or I'm inventing something from a stump,
when that tumble of black branches above it
tilts, resolving into the many-pointed rack
of a bull elk at rest, shifting his head
above his tawny blonde haunches—
tilts, and then tilts back.

Now

we can peer down from space
at the forests, graph
their particular spectrum
of colors, correlate
with ground data
reading the water table,
the moisture in trunk, branch, leaf—
learn what simple rain gauge,
temperature, and wind
or a walk through the woods
have already told—

struggling, tinder-dry, dying,
or slashed and burned—
or burning still—
or walk our streets
and mark where trees
shade our sidewalks,
where roofs receive sun—
though where our children
are safe or unsafe,
our water drinkable,
we need updates,
hour by hour.

Torches

We thought the forests could save us,
storing carbon in their trunks,
pulling down rain from the clouds,
but I read that trees sip water from the soil
like soda straws, and more heat
can increase the pull till columns
of water break,
                air bubbles like emboli
ending the flow, hydraulic fracture,
and what's beyond the break dies
 of thirst even in rain-drenched soil;

or, adapting to drought, trees may close
those small breathing holes in needles
or leaves to keep what little water
they have at the cost of making food—
photosynthesis shut down, they live
on their roots' reserves, saved from thirst
only to starve across the next few years.

Our own breath, too, at risk as new models
show 6 C degrees of ocean warming could end
phytoplankton's bubbling up of oxygen
that supplies two-thirds of ours—loss large
enough to suffocate us all, while we debate
how bad could it be, two more degrees?
              In scorched Tasmania now
the Eucalyptus trees explode, resin
flaming in the wind's hot mouth.

Near-Term Fix

—Drew Shindell's American Geophysical Union's 2012 Talk

I watched online again this week as he named
nine ways to save ourselves, short-term: clean up
the methane from fossil fuels and waste, rice-growing
and manure; replace coal and diesel; end open burning
of wood and waste; buy modern kilns and coke ovens
and clean cook stoves—though the benefits may go
to someone else. How trade less pollution
one place for more rain in another? And what
will persuade all those CEOs of fossil fuels
to stop digging and drilling and fracking and blasting
mountaintops off? What can we offer in trade,
if our beautiful world is not enough?
                                    For Christmas,
I give enough of those clean cooking stoves
for a village, in the names of all my relatives,
find the hundred individual acts that Project Drawdown
lists, leaflet my poet friends, bow in gratitude
to the green leaves of my houseplants—though
now I learn I might better have given up meat,
become vegetarian, kept that old refrigerator.

Why do you find yourself drawn to landscape?

So many ways I tried to bring my father back—
studying the photos of us when he was home
on war leave, me sitting in his lap in my baby fat,
fingering beads, fifteen months, his pipe
in my mouth in one pose, and he is smiling.
I looked for his young face in every college boy,
studied the small print of equations from his books,
but nothing brought him back, and when my heart,
attached to those blank uncomprehending boys,
broke, it was the trees of deep woods that rescued me,
steady by my side all those years—cradle, climb,
shelter, shade; today I try to paint their portraits,
rough bark, curve of limb, their generous leaves.

Clementine Peels

Leathery loose skin of tangerine orange
pulled from the fruit, dragging its fibrous web
of connection like the placenta links womb
and embryo—these mediators between worlds
that swaddle the sweet brief bursts
that feed us—I save the peels, dry
and freeze them, drop them into soups
of winter squash to remind me of a song
my father sang to us in early childhood,
before he was lost and gone, when we
were briefly darlings.

12/22/12
Madison

Dear Ones—this is the day after the end
of the world, Mayan calendar turning over,
12/21/12, like Y2K in our shorter-lived century,
and the poets are meeting to celebrate niches
in our lives for making art—those Edens
behind glass where sunlight stretches
across the floor, those pigeon-holed desks
offering up all the mind's shelved categories,
that long candle-lit table for gathering, the walls
hung with art from many hands—though these
spaces, too, are fragile, ephemeral, arise and vanish,
while all the while our busy traffic, landfill gases,
burning cookfires are somewhere ending the local
worlds we know—our rain and snow, our winds
and soil, our trees and crops, our breathable air,
our drinkable water—so perhaps the doomsayers
were right, though I've rushed out to write checks
for trees and bees in far countries and sit here now
following Walt Whitman's advice to his soul,
tallying Earth's soil, trees, winds, tumultuous waves,
sending in an order for prairie seed, resolving to eat
lentils not beef, take the bus that goes by my door—
refusing the beautiful poetry of grief for the grit
of belief we can push back the date if we choose.

A Local Life

says *The Washington Post* in the obituary
my sister sends—John Hoke, dead at 85,
a tinkerer and inventor we never heard of,
who spent his life seeing solutions everywhere:
solar-powered boats and cars, roof gardens
to cool in summer, heat in winter; yurt
technology only now installed. He stocked
the parks with electric golf carts, turned
the dank stink of sludge ponds into sweet marsh
eco-systems, wanted to bequeath twenty squirrels
to every house, running wheels to generate
what we need of electricity. On the clipping
I try to calculate how many chipmunks
that would convert to, in the spirit of using
our local resource, though the insistent noise
of vocal warning chirps might interfere
with bedtime reading and morning oatmeal.
Over my coffee I read that John Hoke's dead,
and outside our problems multiply—
opportunities, he'd have said.

Contemporary Poetics

The reviewer hates romanticism, and finds
in the poem about scientist Michael Faraday
a brighter future of quantum entanglement
and Heisenberg's Uncertainty Principle
slant in those lines, "marten or hare,"
when any romantic fool musing on
nature would know the difference
between weasel or rabbit tracks. Ack.

Oh future GPS trackers entangled in your
screens, if you come across the scene
of woodland snow crossed *by marten*
or hare, know that the marten, like
the squirrel, bounded with four equal feet
while hare, its back feet bigger than
its front, left larger prints outside
the little ones—
                        and where it is now
not uncertain, its knowledge local,
though you, by now, are everywhere,
and global.

II
The Alphabet of Time

Alphabet

Scribe's invention that makes us able
to call up visions in another's mind, leap
time and space, convey a tale,
a face, a plan, the heart's heat
vibrating in a looped half pleat
of line—look, follow these alpha
to omega runes that abet
memory and sight's pale
hints with sounds turned on the lathe
of words, scribed in the lap
of foolscap from inky bath,
trace of a mind's circuitous path.

Toft Point, Door County

Old-growth balsam shades the shoreline,
soft ground yields underfoot, deadfalls angle
to prevailing winds, and the branches
fill with small restless birds—the turning season
has brought us all north, to that edge
where the hepatica blooms, where whole fields
of pink Arctic primrose star dolomite's white,
the lichens' grey-black. And light, distillate
of a splintered green that has lived through
all the ice and wind a polar winter vortex
brings, cycles now toward a brief, late spring,
pacing us, the warblers, every growing thing.

The Poem You're Carrying With You

Always, at the bottom of thought,
   these stones, beach-strewn,
      picked out by sunlight
        or stumbled upon,
worry stone, memory stone,
   heart stone, some broken-off piece
      of an older world, waiting
        through millions of years
for slow speech, room in your pocket,
   the rub of your thumb, talisman,
      reminder that you're joined
        to every element of earth.

The Invention of Time

At first it was a purely local thought—
sun up, sun down, high noon—
though sun's wanderings taught
the yearly round. *Here*, a split rock
through which light reaches
once more its farthest mark
upon the wall, turning over
all the calendars. And that other
wheel waxing, waning, full,
whose nightly pull marks high tide,
ebb tide, bloodtide as it cycles
through the turning dome of stars,
night sky's chronometer storied
into gods and journeys, plots
and wars—all that looking up
into a mirror of ourselves,
making us want to see what others
see, agree to wear on a wrist
a ticking tock that moves in synchrony
with Coordinated Universal Time—
weighted average of some 300 atomic
cesium clocks' oscillating frequencies—
at 6:36 a.m. this particular day.

5 p.m. May 2, on the way
to the Wisconsin River

Dear Ones—the horizon's
a wash of dark rain
left and right of the road
with a break straight ahead
and we ask—will the sun
thread our journey all the way
to the end, are those rays
of light proof of small gods
pointing the way to the hill
where we plan to camp,
will the sun still be up
to guide us as we pitch
our tent? And will there be
woodcocks courting to buzz
us to sleep?

May 6
Jack's Prairie

Dear Ones—with buckets of seed
mixed with water and vermiculite
we walk the burned acres,
through black nubs of grasses,
listening to loud bird song,
flinging our clutches of dropseed
and sedge, seeding the shade
of the wood edges with trillium
and betony, breathing in the scent
of roasted acorns, circling back
into full sun for baptisia,
rudbeckia, and more—all of us
imagining the sights that will greet us
in the fields of future summers
as one by one a seed takes hold.

So much depends

on an eye for consequence—
hiking down the gravel road
past banks emptied of gentian
and goldenrod, shorn of jewelweed
and vine, cut back to a stubble
of stems and old leaves, we come
to a curve suddenly thick
in maidenhair fern and blue vervain,
Solomon's seal, true and false,
and at its end a Styrofoam plate
nailed on a tree for a sign:
its lettered black command
DO NOT MOW BANK enough
to stop the driver doing his job
for the DNR, saving one
small remnant of the wild.

Showing Up

All these exhortations to show up
at the studio door, the desk, the page—
what's missing still? The willingness
to sit with the everyday—to say
how last night the racket along the road
by the marsh was *Hyla crucifer*—
spring peepers lost in their urgent trilling,
mating songs so loud Will thinks
his tire bearings are giving out—
and we roll down the car windows
to listen to the sound that continues
even though we've stopped.

Bringing Cookies to Chaos

A contradiction in terms, this lecture on chaos
accompanied by cookies, the sweet of butter stirred
into flour, oatmeal, raisins, and chocolate chip,
these turnings and foldings a route to chaos
and batter well mixed, nothing like a dread chasm
opening into a future maw, familiar structures
falling away—but isn't that just the cookie's fate,
baked to crumble in our mouths, even a crumb
lost to a mouse searching the corners of the kitchen
floor later that night? And isn't that the reason
for cookies, anyway, to sweeten the night traveler's
search for a way through the chaotic universe
we tumble through, hoping to be sustained?

Identity Crisis

The Chaos Seminar is spending its summer
in weekly discussion by the lake—Union Terrace,
students sunning, sailboats running, children
climbing the giant chair—and over the din
of asphalt graders and pavement grinders
we're talking about whether any of us
has an identity that persists—or is it
illusion, this *I* of our personal homunculus,
and right off we fall into the pit of existential
crisis, agency one test, continuity another,
the work of the definite article a third,
the Buddhist sects give differing answers,
developmental psychologists parade
the seven—or more—stages of woman
and man, Freudians are splitting the unitary self
into a trinity and a rump group is asking
for a definition of reality and a neighbor
who's joined us is sighing with nostalgia,
remembering the days of his slacker talk youth.

I'm left puzzling over our innocent assumptions—
that I'm an ongoing, sturdy enterprise when, really,
if you tagged each of my molecules radioactively
right now with my name you'd see a sort of cloud,
spreading and dispersing in some long plume
of exhaled breath and sluffed skin, and nothing,
not even my DNA code mutating with the years,
my memory lengthening and lapsing likewise,
nor those name tags zipping through the local
atmosphere, would stay the same, and where's
the *I* in that? Meanwhile the sailboats tack
and turn, each still the same boat the whole hour,
and probably, even the same crew, so far as I know.

Immortality at the Memorial Union

Under the oaks beside the lake,
sparrows busy underfoot,
the topic is how it might
be possible—immortality:
biological engineering
of our telomeres, replacement
of body parts, or virtual life?
Most of the old guys vote
to be downloaded onto
computer chips and continue
indefinitely, pure thought,
bodiless, worldless, checking in
periodically that, yes, indeed,
this is still the self. Just
another big data task.
Others ask more—some
novelty, like a cruise ship's
robotic offerings, a day trip
to a foreign shore or
a simulated smorgasbord.
As for me, it's the living
world I want, the sparrows
and the breeze, and friends
talking under an oak
far older than me.

June 1
Highway N

Dear Ones—behind us, the full moon rose
pewter in the rinsed navy blue; before us,
the setting sun spilled its orange arms
through the oaks, fading as we drove north
to a purple smear of cloud—and then,
faint sideways-visible flash before
we're past, the fawn, standing at
highway's edge in her moon-dappled coat;
what could she, so few days new
to the world, have thought as we sped past?
And I wished hard that whatever she saw
gave her pause to stay there, until
her mother called her back.

Rock and Deer

I dream
the dead-end block
of houses has been razed,
converted back
to woods and wilderness—
the way, last night,
after the echoing booms
and tracers of fireworks,
I saw a mule deer
picking her way
through the snow
under a waning moon
into a new year
of rising temperatures.

In the deep sea, we're told,
hundreds of trillions
of bristlemouth fish
the size of fingers
float about, ghostly lit,
filtering tiny crustaceans
out of the depths
with bristle-like teeth,
while out at the edge
of planetary whirls,
Pluto makes its icy way,
elliptically circling
Frost's question—
what to make
of a diminished thing.

In all the movies
where murder or sex
is not involved
we plan to go

and live on Mars—
planet of rock

and hard knocks,
safer than our city streets
where hearts break
for lives lost,
crushed, dashed.

Somewhere,
wilderness,
and deer,
at home
in the only home
we know.

The Memory Palace

—Do Ho Suh exhibition, MMoCA, 2017

I live in a house made of light,
in the room where the sun
throws open a yellow door at dawn
calling out to plum tree, green grass,
ink rubbed from a stone.

I live in the room where the moon
gazes in like my mother at night,
looking in to see if I've gone to sleep
to the sound of the radiator's heat,
footsteps in the corridor of dream.

I live in a room whose every surface
has been measured and rubbed—house
built from burned hours, afloat
with the beautiful lonesome blues,
jazzman somewhere playing his bass.

I live in the central room of the house
leaning into the light of the refrigerator
whose emptiness can be filled,
imagining colliding worlds, my father
making a home from brushed words.

I live in the house made of light
that remains, that remains, portable
membranes light as spiderwebs and air
stretched across the frame, body
that carries me through my days—

I live in its threads unraveled
nightly in sleep, reassembled
by day as stairs and walls, patterns
of outlets and inlets, flung
gardens, a blossoming branch.

For the End Times

What heals, what carries us through?
Music for the closing of eyes, to carry us
through the dark; and the rise and fall
of remembered words, and companions
on the way, and dreams: I've watched
the emergency crews bear stretchers
out of the house past the children at play
on the doorsteps, shouldered the draped
bodies with my childhood friend, shroud
and box, crypt and fire; armfuls of lilacs
or ashes scattered to lake and woods.
Memory of how each lifted an eyebrow
or laughed or some characteristic shrug
or walk or tilt of head that each would make;
but their songs, the ones that only they
could sing—their songs are done, unless
we learned their tunes: words are not enough.

Holding the emptiness softly

That shower of snow in the lodgepoles
is the raven moving his perch; somewhere
the writer swims her laps in the pool
waiting for plot to catch up to her, the artist
follows her terrier's morning walk to learn
of the passing deer and elk, the jazz composer
sets out to run the trail to the mountain top.
At breakfast the eight-month-old who cried
all night is delighted by the faces of strangers,
his mother close by and sleepless, missing
her former life; and the long-distance runner,
back from the mountain, hears the cycle
of fifths turning its great wheel, like the sun
passing over us all. In the stranded boat
the writer steers into a windy neighborhood,
the stranded islander invents a bookshop
for insomniacs, the new music composer tracks
her fugitive dreams, the science fiction writer
invents a funnier future than the one we face;
the walker considers the heart of her dog,
composes a concert for us all; and the poet
is weeping over the loss of her cats and dogs
long ago. Out of the emptiness of the valley's
begging bowl, something will emerge.

Artists

—after Do Ho Suh's MMoCA exhibit, 2017,
and Paul Lawrence Dunbar's "The Mystery"

First we're nowhere—then here, all eyes
and ears and fingertips measuring this room—
and some future closer than that past, gone again—
how to find our way home? Show me
the time before time began, the evolving play
of everything—but Chaos only shakes
his head and grins. I find no friendly sound
though I put my eyes to all the instruments
of sight, micro-, macro-, telescoping
and satellite—no voice answers back
and daily all these sights vanish in the light
that rises, that daily sets—knowledge
folded away in stitches and woven threads
that one day, too, we must spin out word
by breath, find body and bone dispersed
to time and earth and airy space—forms
with their freight of history scattered across
our century in veils and mystery.

Sept. 25,
Door County

Dear Ones—the moon,
almost full, rises above
the blue horizon,
the pink haze, to scatter
herself like salt
in every ripple and wave,
making a ladder of lenses
by which we could climb
to her if we could walk
on water, if she could enter
the water, if she or we
could make her many
images one with ourselves
and the lake—her shattered
images give hope that we, too,
though scattered through
our days, are whole.

Travel

Bach's Goldberg Variations play
on the new media deck while
the navigation system illuminates
our route and the lady navigator
addresses us formally, *Prepare
to turn off at the right,* reminding
us three times before we exit into
sand country, fields of soybeans,
irrigation rigs scribing their slow
passage, a light blizzard of milkweed
fluff drifting across our view, sandhill
cranes, pair by pair, walking the rows.
All this where once an inland sea
stretched across an unrecorded
landscape. My wish for the world
to come—that Bach still sounds
across green fields. That cranes
still stalk the rows. That milkweed
crowds the ditches. That Monarchs
visit on their way south.

Thanksgiving 2014

Seven thousand miles above the earth
the Van Allen radiation belts deflect
killer electrons that could zap our apps
or body cells, and a vaccine against Ebola
worked this week in twenty volunteers,
though some have aching joints,
and in Ferguson, Missouri, the protesters
still in jail will be released in time
for holiday dinner while we'll sit down
to say thanks for friends, and the work
of scientists, and mourn the country's sons
gunned down, and wonder how we can
deflect the distorting fears, the showdowns,
the stories of them-or-us that infect us now.

Blood orange

fits in the palm, heavy, its sweet interior
red as its name, some mutation that doubles
its anthocyanin. Once it happened in Sicily,
a century that Muslims and Christians
lived in peace—Inquisition come and gone
already; once it happened in California,
just before the first war of that century;
it might happen again, this beautiful chance
increasing the sweetness of life; I mean
this to be a gift held out in my hand to you—
this descendant of a seldom-repeated event
threading its weight through our days:
its juice blameless and dripping in our hands.

III
Gravitational Waves

Gravitational Waves

So gravity, too, comes in units,
and when we exploded to cosmos,
its jerky progression left bumps
in the background hum—a music
like notes on the scale with intervals
between that rippled into time
and space as they inflated to make
a start on life as we know it now
or so I was thinking last year, reading
we've seen the signature of gravity
waves, five sigma certain, after
staring three frozen years into space
from the South Pole at the background
microwave residue that's as far back
as we can go—creation story for children
of bomb blast and rock and roll.
Though now those bumps
are consigned to galactic dust,
and we go back to staring though it
at colliding black holes,
waiting to be six sigma sold,
a date that arrives in 2016,
headlines blazing that Einstein
was right a hundred years ago.

Mastodon Bones, Colorado

At Snowmass, the machines dig up
the bones of more than thirty mastodons,
every age in a family group, scattered
in the same Ice Age layer on a glacial
lakeshore. The NOVA program's scientists
experiment with a sand box, toy elephant,
to show us how an earthquake could turn
the shore to quicksand, liquefy the place
they stood, sinking up to their knees
or bellies—and moments later reverse
to solid mud, trap them for the weeks
it took to starve, whole families, shoulder
to shoulder—I shudder, imagining
the sound of families calling out
to one another across the many hours.

The Chaos Seminar Considers Artificial Intelligence

Will robotic intelligence be the end of us, the seminar
wants to know, and when will we get self-driving cars
and robotic dogs for the elderly? Google Translate
fattens on a billion phrases to make the matches
that equate *The spirit is willing but the flesh is weak*
in English and Russian seamlessly cognate—when
fifty years ago back-translation assured *The wine
is fine but the meat is rotten* and we knew it would
never happen, too much to learn for our lifetime,
no machine could beat a human player of chess or go.
Now comes the magnitude of memory and speed
it takes, and the record of whole lives, literatures,
to simulate eye and mind and world until it's not
a cartoon show but a replacement for us: it needs
a heart, and gut instincts, still, and instructions
for how to decide, in an imminent crash, who will live
and who will die: and will those rules also apply
to instructions to preserve our one green planet?

Reimagining the Past of My Hometown

What if seventy-five years ago the Army Engineers
had built a town with no Gamble Valley Rd.
leading into shacks with oilcloth windows,
a segregated slum? What if the city
and state had barred no one from an education,
home, or bathroom? What if no husband shot Ida
in her leg, leaving a wound that wouldn't heal?
What if no fist broke Winifred's checkbone,
what if she could have afforded to have it fixed?
What if no John Birchers burned crosses
on crab grass lawns, preached hate?
What if all us of had ridden in the back of the bus,
unpacking our sandwiches to share
with whoever was there?

You are not alone

Every tree on earth
is your companion
in the breathing air.
Every wild bee and butterfly
at work in your asters
knows your face and scent.
Every bird in the arborvitae trees
knows the sound of your footsteps,
carrying seed to the feeders.
Every chipmunk in your yard
drinks from the water you pour
each morning into the bowl,
as do the glossy green-black grackles,
the many sparrow families,
the jays in their brilliant suits
of white, black and blue,
the cardinals in their reds.
And those you pass in greeting
on the street, walking their small
or large dogs, coaxing them
to move on from the scents
of last night, are your friends,
and in front of the school,
the child crossing guards
waving their flags for you.

Artist's Statement

You see my work on the wall there—
I started late, painted what I saw—
saw, and loved, though I can't say how
or why—and lacking art, made by hand
in a kind of dance, gesture pointing *here*
and *here*, not anything itself but the smell
of phlox and beebalm in the air, the blue
of sky against the maple's turning leaves—

made what I felt, which, I see now,
reading books on making art, lacks focal point
when *all, all this* is what I meant; lacks,
too, contrast in value, light against dark,
when all of it was *bright, bright*, and no
leading lines to guide the eye, when what
I meant was *earth and sky, path and tree,*
dancer and bouquet—and though

I tried I couldn't show the motion of every
littlest thing, bee or hummingbird,
that caught my eye. I wanted to paint it all,
every leaf shaking slightly in the wind,
its toothed edge and veins, the twigs,
their scars and buds, the furrowed bark,
the stretch of summer forest reaching back
and back, beyond the river where the ripples

caught the colors of the veins of stones,
the spill of water—the shadows moving
in the underbrush, quick and indistinct,
that speak of life beneath the paint.
Perhaps it's only color I've sometimes
found, the way the sky vibrates against
maple's red—and memories of works
recalled, Matisse, Bonnard, Monet.

The Chaos Seminar Takes on Climate Change

"The future is already here—it's just unevenly distributed"
—attributed to William Gibson, The Economist, 2003

What to do? we debate, arrayed around round tables
by the lake, an algae-green in late summer heat,
meeting Bernard's challenge to understand
how fast we're trashing our only planet,
and I pass around a list of things we could do,
a hundred different actions, Project Drawdown—
indeed, we've bought the efficient new humidifier,
refrigerator, turned down the thermostat—
We're a complex system, says Clint, *don't sweat
the details, kill the nearest snake. Something
will emerge that looks like a plan, looking back;
structures of action are chaotic* and I'm left asking
how to keep heart—police arrayed against
the water keepers, hate preached by the trumped-up
candidate—oh, be fierce for what's at stake:
bread and water and our future life together.
Be fierce on the side of love!

Lake Farm Park
Sept. 8, 2016

Dear Ones—clouds and sun
over the water-soaked ground
after three inches of rain—the lake
full to the brim, the painters quiet
as we paint the lake, and only
a little riffle of water as the wind
spends its energy in the cottonwoods
frantically waving their leaves—
I feel so lucky, as autumn descends
and green retreats, to know that, rising
in the channels of each tall trunk,
drunk up in roots, the rain is stored—
as this hour of quiet and shaking leaves,
of losing ourselves in sight, is ours.

Notebook

—after W.S. *The Joy of Writing*

How old-fashioned to sit
with a palm-sized notebook
writing cursive with my pen—
my only app an agile mind,
warmed in early morning gym—
well, at least, a little less stiff,
after lifting legs and weights—

I imagine Szymborska's company,
wryly listing philosophies—
but now, searching for her words
in memory, I'm wishing
for a Google portal
into the hive-mind world,
where unforgettably she says

The twinkling of an eye will take as long as I say
and will, if I wish, divide into tiny eternities,
full of bullets stopped in mid-flight.

though neither this pen
nor those weights will stop
the clock that ticks our lives,
those bullets in flight,
whatever we wish,
whatever we write.

Message to My Future Self

Ok, this is a bad day, a bully
put in charge of the nation,
temperature climbing; yours,
I hope, better, in that future
I've piled my fears into—is it
so bad, being old-old-old?
Is the weather as hot as we all
predicted?

Are you living in a tent city,
queuing for water, wearing
a mask in the choking haze
of forest fire, or jammed
on board a boat, hoping for
entry on a foreign shore,
the way it is now for so many?

Do you remember me
and all my worries? Look,
I've brought you chocolate,
from the days when it was cheap,
and music, the rock and roll
of your generation, and Pete
Seeger and the Beetles, Baez
and Collins and Denver,

and a slide show of all
the paintings we painted
and poems we made and photos—
so many—of the people
we loved—here's your son
John, playing his bass, your son
Josh, with his newest painting—
but perhaps you're not

rocking in front of a window
watching the squirrels but out
planting prairie seed or gathering
kale for a salad or practicing
sun salutes though your toes
are creaky—or working a puzzle
with your ancient husband—wiser
than I am now, less worried;

or, if I'm a stranger, enjoy
this green tea, this dark chocolate,
Pete singing, *We are the boat*,
tell me again how you rescued
the kittens in the iris garden, how
your mother braided your hair
every day into long French braids.

I draw the card Responsibility

So many syllables, unlike Joy
or Play, so many steps to take
in the dark, guarding my brother,
at four, myself, a big girl of six,
from robbers and creatures
that roam in the night—I lay
awake, wide-eyed, in the big bed
keeping watch, reciting the phone
number in my head of the neighbors
where my parents had walked
to play cards—first of the nights
I knew that it all depended
on me; or the assignment, later,
standing at the oven door watching
the brown sugar bubble on toast
in the light of the broiler, trying
to time just enough for crust, before
the edges darkened to charcoal;
or later, at Girl Scout camp, to watch
the campfire, towering log cabin
inferno, and sweep the sparks
back into the flames.

Did you know I loved you?

Even more than I loved the blue lights
flickering on that first Christmas tree,
or the dolls from France that stood
beneath—you were my bluebirds,
my tarot cards, my banana trees—
exotic tropical paradise we landed in
during the war years, tatting on the arms
of the chairs and hollyhocks by the fence,
my lucky rabbit foot you took away
to keep the fever from infecting me—
sometimes I'm afraid. Have another
pancake, this small orange, some
imaginary tea. I just followed the recipe—
pour something in, stir, and serve—
and when I did get sick, ear drum inflamed
like a hornet nest's attack, each
with a different face, you plunged me
into icy water wrapped in icy sheets,
took me to the hospital's white bed,
its empty days and nights with penicillin
sting. Sometimes I'm afraid. Sometimes
I watch the squirrels leaping
in the snow. Mostly, I remember
the lights—that blue like tropical
nights!—the way they shone
at night over banana trees.

Petition

I'm full of opinions about how
to run the world, signing petitions

every day to Congress and businesses
to save the whales—or birds—or wolves

to save the mountains—or rivers—or lakes—
to save our rainforest, glaciers, children—

to put an end to war and tax havens
for the rich and assault rifles for the populace

to make voting fair and give women
equal rights and pay and choices—

Black Lives Matter! Fund Planned Parenthood!
Welcome immigrants! End bigotry! My petitions

rain in a digital blur on lawmakers
bought by top dollar capitalists

cruising Caribbean shores—my names
on so many rolls—joined with yours

and yours and yours—we're uncountable
now; better to petition the stars to shine,

to ask the leaves of the trees to breathe
in and out of their many small mouths,

to pull water out of the ground,
up their long, corded arteries, to shade

the rivers running their courses; to plead
with the rain—the rain!—to fall—

and then with wet faces to watch over
the small creatures that cross

the field in the dark, each carrying a seed
in its mouth under the silent owl.

"All sketches wish to be real"

—T. Tranströmer

I followed with my brush
the dark spine of her fur,
the outline of her ears,
the way her jaw moved
rhythmically, black chin
beneath black nose, the jut
of her shoulder, large dark eyes—
only a watercolor sketch
of a deer on a postcard now,
but in my memory
of moving eye and hand,
she's real.

Haibun with Hafiz

—The words you speak become the house you live in.

Not a mule deer sighted yet, the day a thin gray
mist; cold sun, and all the oldest lodgepoles
standing dead or dying around the studios as I
pass the sap orange and blue-gray fungus scrolling
their scaling trunks, their clusters of red needles
catching light. Branched bones reach out of snow,
skeletons of last year's cuts. I walk the tracks, at
least, of deer, the path of the martens' bounding
circuit, artists on their way to work, cabin by
cabin; breathe in the haze of day; move in chi
gong dance with sky, the dim outline of the
mountains. Tiny flakes slant across my sight.
Passing Studio Valentine I hear a composer trying
tone rows on the piano.

Lemon sun, the few
falling flakes, a path of tracks—
a new concerto.

Lost all this morning in a maze of news

while outside at 30 below the snow on the trees
shone violet to the blue sky and lemon light
sparkled in a few blowing ice crystals.
Where was I? Circling the moon—its craters
within craters and knobby mountains.
Following the fading of the mangrove forests
that shield the Bengal tigers. Watching
from space the wildfires burning up Australia.
Reading the short story about feminine
product executives in a creativity workshop.
Blood, sweat, and tears; fire and forests
and rock. Considering the wikiHow steps
of a meditation on the body: add bones
and marrow, nerve and sinew, tendons,
fat, organs, senses, cells—lost in mitochondria
while the sun dropped its shining face
behind the mountains, sun's large arc
what turns the small.

Rainer Maria Rilke, I am revising my life

I am going to give up protecting territory
that is no longer mine, cede it to the young
bright-eyed ones who are reinventing wheels
I have personally reinvented myself
and I am going to give up draping myself
every morning in the crepe of the terrible
things that have happened everywhere
on earth since I went to sleep unless
there's a step I can take and I am going to
give up staring into my computer screen
in the vain hope of human connection
or news with some investigative depth
or friendly entertainment and I am going
to walk out for exercise class at sun-up
or even before saying *Yes*! to bicep curls
and triceps stretches and the plank
held for a whole minute—well, at least
forty seconds—and thence with my love
to the community gardens where, among
the goldfinch and blackbird flocks,
the heavy hanging sunflower heads,
the red fists of cabbage beginning to peek
out and all the small drupelets making up
each raspberry reddening in early light
and the heritage green beans continuing
their astounding lengthening with no
strings attached, still tender and green
in old age, we will harvest our breakfast
and winter meals. I'll even try to work up
to you, William Stafford, writing the poems
that come in the dream space at 4 am,
before first morning light.

Waiting to hear two great poets read

we scan our cell phones, flight delays,
    check-in times in this window between
spring blizzards—we've seen them
    over our wine and pizza holding forth
at a long table, wheel-chaired, white-haired,
    while we talked to young students
and assistant profs, catching up on lives;
    our speakers have a Nobel apiece,
and words that I hear daily on the CD
    in my Mazda Protégé, where Heaney's
the *palpable lithe otter of memory*
    replays between the piper's tunes,
sounds from Beowulf challenging Yeats,
    and Walcott, our other poet, has taken on
Odysseus, his departure and return remade
    for Caribbean times; five thousand
of us, a tribe, wait to hear our elders vie
    to translate lives to words
that might be spoken centuries from now—
    poems that burn in memory,
given only to a few: we're just in time.
    Six months later, Heaney, dying,
texts his last words to his wife:
    noli timere—don't be afraid—
and now Walcott has set out
    on that same journey.

The Egg and I

Will dreams he's found the perfect egg,
after so many almost-theres pulled from rivers,
culled from beaches, piled in baskets
in our living room, and given this rare stone
to me, and asks what have I done with it?
I see it, elevated to Renaissance frame,
a tiny brush stroking on layer after layer
of light and shadow in creamy oils the way
the YouTube artist painted, as we watched in class,
its perfect ovoid shape and slightly pebbled
surface rising from the strokes of paint—
or no, the light reflected from the paint—
and feel its weight in my hand, a freight
of something new, life beginning again,
and what have I done with it? he asks,
and holding it warm and heavy in my palm,
this egg, I feel it break open, hatching a universe
where each of us joins together in a circling dance—
light winking across the void its filament—

The Docent of Tide Pools
—for Betsy

The Dean has retired to take up
a dream job, part-time, odd hours,
leading the curious to inspect
small worlds, showing them how
the anemones wait for the rising tide
to flower and feed with their stinging
barbs and spiny sea urchins watch
for unwary prey, their whole body
one alert eye, and starfish inch by inch
scrub the rock clean of life and kelp
and sea cucumbers dazzle and dance
when the tide is in and barnacles,
like old academicians, cling
tenaciously to place—the rounds
of grazing and basking and display
different on every visit, the whole
chaotic and precarious world
as vibrant as any university.

The Company of Spoons

Close-companioned, curled up
belly to back, on our sides—
"spooning," the old books called it,
sometime after the bundling boards
were taken away—like those that might
have once been found In Iceland's
early centuries; tourists, we walked
through their old sod farmhouses,
imagined the animals housed under
the floorboards for creature warmth,
their breath rising to heat the whole family
and all the farmhands dormitory-housed
in pairs on beds ranged down the room,
only the farmer and his wife with privacy,
shivering behind a curtain; rosemaled
trunks at the foot of each bed,
each sleeper settled to rest like spoons
in the wooden drawer—warm,
and quiet if they stirred in the dark.

Flame

Sometime in your eighties or nineties
     the ruin might begin—
a little getting lost, a word here
     and there avoiding the light,
just out of sight—but then
     a memory clear as a bell
for your eight-year-old birthday,
     your yellow pinafore
and the taste of the yellow cake
     with its chocolate frosting
and the crepe paper streamers
     sticky and your brother blowing
that whistle that curls out like a tongue—
     the day flares up in the house,
candles still burning.

Looking Back

It's not true
    that I was always lost.
I found my way
    more than once—
through ravine and briar patch
    to elementary school,
cross-town on foot
    between the homes
to visit friends
    on the roads
I'd learn to drive
    in a 1950s Ford
with '51 front end,
    feeling the thrill
of controlling
    a power greater
than my own
    and heading out of town
though now I try
    to find the words
that will make a map
    to take me back
and it's all ravine
    and briar patch
and an old Ford
    burning oil.

White Canoe

—after Peter Doig's painting

Where do we go when we die?
That frail craft of body
drifting on the dark lake,
woods rising up from the far shore,
stars falling through rippling water,
light scattered from the sentinel trees,
multiplied, refracted, in the lens of the night—
white emptiness of boat and below,
hazy, reversed, the soul,
that bird of passage carrying the whole
into the echoes of all we know.

All Souls Day

Dear Ones—I've pasted
your photographs on the wall,
folded you into old albums,
not really believing you'd go,
wishing I had sent word before
to say that I loved you, that all
my life as a child your lives
were firelight and lamp to me,
the clink of convivial glasses,
the dance and the talk I stood
watching—you taught me gossip
and art, brandy old-fashioneds
and sermons, powerboating
and softball, early morning
weeding and finger painting,
ballet and piano and the Wizard
of Oz and mystery story
reading, scrubbed floors and
Green stamp pasting, the running
stitch of the Singer Sewing machine,
the importance of letter writing—
all you who were young, then,
and impatient and loving,
all you missing ones,
all you I'm missing.

Highlights

Marks that catch the eye first and lead it round:
that spark of life in Vermeer's girl—eye, pearl, lip—
or the patches of white in Renoir's *Girl*
with a Watering Can, or the blank white of the watercolor
sheet that you must take forethought for to show
how light falls brightest here, and there; or the space
at the end of a line of poetry that offers time
as the mind travels for you to imagine why
the girl in the pearl earring is speaking to you,
now that you've met her eyes.

Ephemeral

This is the day you surfed the web
for news of Justin Bieber, trying
to catch up with culture, face-booked
your breakfast of eggs-over-easy,
raspberries in yoghurt, bookmarked
the great blue heron cam, ditto the puppies
saved from the trash and Leonard Cohen
singing Hallelujah at various husky-voiced
ages, scanned the science news for news
of compounds that cure cancer in mice
or start the protein-folding error that spreads
exponentially through the brain of same,
cures promised as the outcome in every
press release, then settled in to AARP's
free-cell solitaire, its satisfying stacks
piled into sorted suits as you deploy
the mouse, and then a sideways glimpse
of the weather of the day on NOAA's
radar site—though when you exit
to the kitchen and another cup of coffee
before tackling the morning news
and email box, you see that clouds
have already blocked the sun, and rain
is falling steadily on the landscape
you planned to paint today.

Cows Lying Down in the Long Spring Grass
Under the Afternoon Sun on the Way to The Clearing

Just after Rosendale and the shark-nose car
of the traffic cop lurking behind the bar
on Route 26 we pass them—Holsteins,
Guernseys, faced every which way, legs
folded under, the green grass so thick
they seem to float, all gazing out on the heaven
their field has become, chewing their cud—
oh we too plan to plunge into a trillium-lit
woods with our tribes of writers, wildflower
walkers, fused glass makers and watercolor
artists, come home only at noon to draw
ourselves up to willowware, handmade tables,
bright red strawberries, pitchers of fudge.

If I Ran the Government: My Plan
To Rescue the Economy and Create Jobs

I'd mandate that every child at birth
would be issued a triangle and drum,
a xylophone, maraca, and accordion;
a violin and Suzuki lessons at three,
and a piano in every living room for mom
and a sousaphone or sax for dad;
and for first grade, a recorder or flute
—which would require whole new college
departments and professors of Suzuki method
and band conducting and teachers of dance,
new factories for the making of musical
instruments and soundproofing rooms
and sound cancelling headphones,
new construction workers and architects
and engineers to build new band shells
and concert halls and dance floors
and folding chairs and barbecues,
a whole fashion industry focused on
band uniforms and tutus, flamenco dresses
and tap shoes, and orchestral commissions
for thousands of new works
—it would be a buildup second only
to our history of weaponry, fallout
a whole industry of export dulcimers
and luthiers, piano tuners and repairmen,
and dance music would ring out
on every street corner where walkers
could join in jigs and reels, clogging
and mazurkas, Cajun waltzes, solving
incidentally the obesity and loneliness
epidemics while a whole folkloric
research enterprise would spring up
recording the history and spread
of variant versions, and music camps

and festivals year round would pump
money into depressed pubs and Kansas
storefronts and New England hamlets
—and that's just the start: add art,
and we'll be talking global.

Poem to be read when you encounter a wall stretching for hundreds of miles—

Begin the plans to plant suitable vines—
clematis, or trumpet vine, bougainvillea,
or grapes; wisteria, honeysuckle, or jasmine;
having enlisted their unstoppable forces
to climb the wall, lay tile for plazas
on either side, form tables and chairs
from wrought iron, or pinyon pine,
choose the places for farmers' markets,
pave the paths that will carry the carts
of red and green peppers, hot or sweet;
baskets of cheeses, eggs, cornbread,
greens; and hire the string bands,
mariachi bands, accordion players
to perform in the shadows and when
you have lined up the food carts,
the flower venders, the portrait artists,
carve the windows, looking through
to the sellers and singers and dancers
on the other side: then take out the saws
and cut out the doors for the longest
continuous sidewalk feast, music,
and dance celebration in our world:
attraction as great as China's Great Wall,
Australia's Great Barrier reef, though
really, the stalls and the people are all
that you need, not a wall at all.

The Internet of Things

—"is far bigger than anyone realizes."
Wired Magazine

You too can be swept into the crosstalk
of your refrigerator reporting you're out
of milk and your smartwatch making
a shopping list and on your run your heart
monitor will demand a faster pace
and your all-weather solar-powered fleece
ask for the sunny side of the street
as the driverless cars zipping past
detect you pausing at the crosswalk
and a buzzer sounds to tell you its time
to cross now and you can retire free will
and thought as your comparison shopping
app selects the nearest cheapest store
for organic leeks and heavy cream
while your weight watching app scrambles
to substitute low-fat organic Greek yogurt
and recompute your trajectory back home
where you'll dine with a friend half-way
around the world gazing at each other
in your refrigerators' polished doors
over vichyssoise and a just-in-time wine
delivered by drone from the vineyard.

"If you were shrunk to the size of a pencil and put in a blender, how would you get out?"

—Goldman Sachs question for job candidates

I try to imagine myself young, hip, business-schooled,
    suited and heeled, hungry for money, looking
at the interviewer on whom my future depends, choosing
    my path—thinking *are you out of your mind?*
as I coo *Hey, just the kind of challenging job I like?*
    Make a rope of my clothes and use my heels
for a grappling hook, shouting the while *pull the plug*!?
    Jam the blender with a briefcase of cash?
Or cut to the metaphorical chase, ask for a bail-out
    with a bonus to cushion my life as purée?
But my friends have better answers, clearly cut out
    for the job: jamming the pencil in the blade
and using it and the blender's glass grid to chimney
    up the wall they way they have in Canyonland,
or consulting arcane knowledge of the effects
    of scale on leaping power, point out
that if you were that small, you could probably
    leap out, leaving the pencil to jam
future threats to job candidates or milkshakes
    for the corporate clan.

Spaceship Earth

The cult that runs
the only good organic restaurant
with Wi-Fi for miles around
is studying in earth school
how they might employ
their future super powers
in the next world, which
gives me pause, but
their whole wheat Belgian waffles
and thick blueberry syrup
are clearly to die for, and they're not,
so far as I can tell, planning
to take passengers.

The Science Daily News, August 25, 2016

Here, my go-to site for respite from the rising temperatures
of rhetoric and fear, I find, astonishingly, the headline
"Saving the planet from climate change with a grain of sand"
and find they mean it: the smallest crystals of silicone,
3.5 nanometers wide, capable of harvesting sunlight
through all its lengths to make carbon monoxide
out of CO_2—which, if it doesn't suffocate us, will make
great fuel—and all evening I swim through hope, praise
for a Canadian university, U of Toronto, fixed on finding
ways to simultaneously pull CO_2 out of the atmosphere
and replace our fossil fuel—recycling on a global scale—
though as my laps add up I begin to worry all over again—
will greed deplete so much of air that trees begin
to suffocate? Where will all those pilot plants be located
and how fast does weather mix the air and just how
does carbon monoxide become a fuel and who owns
the patent and what will the coal miners and oil frackers
do now that we might want them to keep on removing
mountaintops and injecting water tables and adding
the CO_2 that we've come to depend on for our fuel?
And what vast consortium of government bureaucracies
will spring up to titrate livable, breathable, usable air,
and will the sands of Sahara and Australia become
as valuable as oil and who will remember the living earth?
Though today, I let hope walk with me, praise
ingenuity, technology, and civilization, imagine
a decade coming of sand and solar powered cars
self-driving down our arterial roads, scarfing up
the carbon dioxide, pulling down the temperature.

Wrens in Our Watering Can

I want to write about two wrens
who are busily bringing insects
to our copper watering can
hanging under the eaves—
they've filled it with sticks
and now, by the sound, nestlings,
who must be growing minute
by minute in the metallic dark
while mother and father take turns
accompanying them or bringing in
bugs or singing from a nearby tree—

I want to write about the wrens
who enliven our days with coming
and going and song but my country
is tearing children from parents
and caging them, alone, terrified,
among strangers, and I say to you,
sir, who ordered this misery, and you
who have carried out these orders,
and you, reaping the profit per child,
if children were wrens, the parents
would have pecked out your blind eyes.

Stepping out of the meeting,
our spinning energy of a week's workshop

slowing, I watch the white breath of the snow
lift into mist, erase the mountains

the sound of a train threads the clouds,
bearing logs or oil out of hearing

all week we have been listening to the echoes
of numbers, one hundred ways to solve cubic roots

tucking laser-cut spirals into globes
imagining hypercubes

assembled by pairs, parenthetically
reminded that every opening must have its closing

computed the relative risk
of being the victim of a mass shooting

or catastrophe in an old pine forest
the dynamics of a heart attack

the mist that rises becomes the cloud descending
sometimes we forget the mountain

Acknowledgments

My great thanks to the Banff Centre for Arts and Creativity for space in the Leighton Studios to work on these poems; to the members of my two writing groups of long years, Marilyn Annucci, the late Susan Elbe, Catherine Jagoe, Jesse Lee Kercheval, Sara Parrell, Alison Townsend; Lenore Coberly, Alice D'Alessio, CX Dillhunt, Jeri McCormick, Richard Roe, Lynn Patrick Smith, Karen Updike; to poets Sandra Stark and Susan Wicks; and to the following journals:

About Place Journal: Reimagining the Past of My Hometown; Dear Ones, Banff, Jan. 16.

Appalachia: Light; The Poem You're Carrying with You; Dear Ones, 5 p.m. May 2, on the way to the Wisconsin River; Toft Point, Door County; Dear Ones, May 6, Jack's Prairie.

Ascent: Showing Up; Holding the Emptiness Softly.

Canary: Dear Ones, June 1, Highway N; So much depends.

Common Online: Immortality at the Memorial Union; Blood Orange.

The Dalhousie Review: Clementine Peels.

Do Ho Suh Exhibit, Madison Museum of Contemporary Art: Circles; Artists: The Memory Palace.

Flyway: Identity Crisis; The Invention of Time.

Hawk and Handsaw: Dear Ones, Jan. 6, Banff; Dreams of the Science Writers' Workshop; Dear Ones, Dec. 25, Banff.

JOMP21, Dear Mr. President, Chicago Poetry Press, 2018: Poem to be read when you encounter a wall stretching for hundreds of miles.

Midwest Prairie Review: Cows Lying Down in the Long Spring Grass Under the Afternoon Sun on the Way to The Clearing.

Nimrod: Rock and Deer.

Off the Coast: Why do you find yourself drawn to landscape?

Slippage: The Docent of Tide Pools.

Switched-On Gutenberg: Dear Ones, Jan. 18, Banff.

Talking Writing: Stepping out of the meeting, our spinning energy of a week's workshop; A Local Life.

Terrain: Dear Ones, 12/22/12, Madison.

Tamsen: The Tension of Opposites.

Valparaiso Poetry Review: White Canoe.

Verse Wisconsin: If I Ran the Government: My Plan to Rescue the Economy and

Create Jobs.

Wisconsin Poets Calendar, 2016: Dear Ones, Sept. 25, Door County.

Written River: January; A warm wind.

TEBOT BACH
A 501 (c) (3) Literary Arts Education Non Profit

THE TEBOT BACH MISSION: advancing literacy, strengthening
community, and transforming life experiences with the power of poetry
through readings, workshops, and publications.

THE TEBOT BACH PROGRAMS
1. A poetry reading and writing workshop series for venues such as homeless
shelters, battered women's shelters, nursing homes, senior citizen daycare
centers, Veterans organizations, hospitals, AIDS hospices, correctional
facilities which serve under-represented populations. Participating poets
include: John Balaban, Brendan Constantine, Megan Doherty, Richard Jones,
Dorianne Laux, M.L. Leibler, Laurence Lieberman, Carol Moldaw, Patricia
Smith, Arthur Sze, Carine Topal, Cecilia Woloch.

2. A poetry reading and writing workshop series for the Southern California
community at large, and for schools K-University. The workshops have featured local,
national, and international teaching poets; David St. John, Charles Webb, Wanda
Coleman, Amy Gerstler, Patricia Smith, Holly Prado, Dorothy Lux, Rebecca Seiferle,
Suzanne Lummis, Michael Datcher, B.H. Fairchild, Cecilia Woloch, Chris Abani, Laurel
Ann Bogen, Sam Hamill, David Lehman, Christopher Buckley, and Mark Doty.

3. A publishing component to give local, national, and international poets
a venue for publishing and distribution.

Tebot Bach
Box 7887
Huntington Beach, CA 92615-7887
714-968-0905
www.tebotbach.org